Hidden Harmony

Ekaete Ekop

Published in 2020 by FeedARead.com Publishing
Copyright © Ekaete Ekop

A CIP catalogue record for this title is available from the British
Library.

Book design: Whitedove Publicity Limited
Photo credits: Ekaete Ekop

To my parents:
Dr Albert C. Ekop and
Mrs. Martina A. Ekop.
You are The Best.
One of a kind.
You created a home that
encouraged us to see in
new ways and to
question the seeming
'obvious'.

Contents

FOREWARD

'I KNEW my vocation…I would name things and call them to another life.' That is precisely what Dr Ekaete Ekop has done with these splendid poems. When one reads them, ordinary things become different, become fresh, glow with Being, as seen through the prism of Mindfulness. Problems become opportunities; scars become story lines; failures, precious experiences.

These extraordinary lines draw together insights from every sphere of lifesocial, medical, spiritual, environmental'matching experience with knowledge', as one of the poems says in another context.

The poems on these pages are a smile from the heart and, as Ekaete says, 'a smile from the heart never hurts'. Indeed, it heals. Which is what these poems do, in an utterly astonishing way.

David Rice
16 April 2020
Director: Killaloe Hedge-School of Writing,
Ireland

Baptism
spree

He had been away over a year.
It was a long time,
We had missed him.
When he walked into the compound
There were cheers and whistles -
Bobo was home, our Bobo had returned.

Our Bobo was Bobo from his hair tips
To the nail on his little toe.
From his smile to his wink to his stories;
From his angry scowl to his wangering gait
Bobo-ish in everything.
All his expressions
Bearing the engrave of his person.

We sat and listened and teased;
We laughed, we reminisced, we re-unioned.
But we could see - Bobo was…different
He did not tell many stories.
He listened, he asked,
he questioned, he enquired
he drew forth our stories
our deepest cries, our highest glories.
His eyes oozed compassion
His attention conveyed hidden knowing
Bobo was different, but he was still ours.

8

Late that night,
the crickets chirping
And a few of us still left
He told us.
He did.
He had been baptized.

Baptized? What was that?
Who did it to you? Was it painful?
How long did it take?
Was it like cocaine, or a scolding?
Or a massage?

He smiled at the questions
He tried to explain, to clarify
He had been immersed
And fresh power flowed through him
He had a new name
He was living this new name
The name lived through him.
It made no sense…at first

But you are still Bobo?
We sought reassurance
Well---it is part of my unfolding
Now I live from the place
of my new name Nuru
I…am light.

How does it work?
This new name now works for you?
Or you work for it?
Neither I only allow its life-force
Flow in and through me
I am….light.

For days I mulled, I mused, I pondered.
Just like that?
Bobo was now Nuru
In his smile, his wink, his choices,
A new life lived as Bobo,
I mean, Nuru.
All expressions Nuru-ish.

Then lightening pierced
My incubating darkness.
I knew my vocation!
To be a Baptizer.
I would name things,
And call them to another life
By God's power in which I am.

I set the date, the time, the ritual
I chose the place, the centrepiece, the colour theme
I was the baptizer and the witnesses
My inner drums rolled
The ceremony began

I renamed Problem, Opportunity
My Debts became Providence Receptacles
My Scars, Story Lines
Failures were baptized Precious Experiences
My Heap of Dirty Laundry, Textile Diversity

Loneliness became Rich Solitude
Betrayals were Emotional Spring Cleaning
Insomnia was named Clandestine Encounterwith the
  Divine.
My Uncooperative Office-Mate
was now my Patience Coach.
I was on a baptizing spree!
Breathing new meaning into obsolete experiences

Miraculously my life is re-christened
Each day an experimental adventure
I no longer 'do laundry'
I 'recycle my pile of Textile Diversity'
Oh so interesting!
God bless Bobo…or Nuru
He had revealed to me my innate power

I give new names to old games
And like a football referee
Nothing is 'foul' until I say so
I award myself the penalties, the goals, the free kicks.
Nobody blows the whistle in my game
But me.

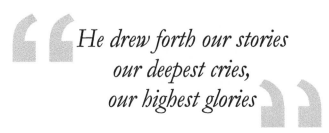

He drew forth our stories
our deepest cries,
our highest glories

2

They lied to me?

What is this dark place?
What is this frightening silence?
Why the solitude?
Alone. Alone. All alone.

Wet. Cold. Heavy.
Why the absence of light?
Why the companionship of gloomy thoughts?
Alone. Alone. All alone.

Is this the death they spoke of?
They said it was a transition.
But this is no threshold
This is the end....the termination
The conclusion. It is over.

They said I should let go
I should yield control
Let go of my plans, my ideas, my wise blueprint
And fall into Something bigger than me
Something infinite
"Unless a grain of wheat dies..."

They said it would be glorious
Magnificent. Full of splendour.
They lied. Oh, they lied to me.
I am disintegrating, decomposing
There is nothing. Nada.
I am disappearing
Reverting to nothing. Painfully
I don't recognise me...

But.... wait!
If I am disintegrating...who is the 'I'
That witnesses the disappearance?
Who is the 'I' that does not recognise 'Me'?
Am 'I' two? Or one? Or legion?

I am changing, something is new-ing
Is it 'I' or 'Me'?
What is this freshness beginning?
In this putrid decay?
And who witnesses this?
How is it witnessed in abject solitude?

What is happening?
In this drama scene,
I am both actress and audience
What is this mystery unfolding?

Ah! Aah! Aaaah!
I Am both; and more!
The 'I' that I Am does not die
That Eternal Onlooker
That witnesses the Me
As it changes form
Over and over

One form in darkness, one form in light
One manifestation in the clouds
Another in the ocean bed
Like the Pillar of Cloud
And the Pillar of Fire
And death, yes death, the interface
One I. Many Me's

Always the 'I'
Playing with options
The 'I'
Immortal, Invincible, Diverse
The Kaleidoscope of Being
Life in abundant possibilities.

...fall into
Something
bigger than me

3

Sap
Alive

This living sap within
With a life and mind of its own
Creating its own channels
Seeking avenues out

Sometimes oozing slowly
Like toothpaste from a tube
Or flowing in rhythm
Like soft waterfalls
Sometimes coursing wildly
Like angry floods

Sometimes sitting still
Like frozen lakes in winter
Sometimes raging in circles
Like hurricanes and tornadoes

Sometimes flowing in one direction
Obedient to exact laws
Sometimes pitting currents
Against itself
As in a cockfight

Always searching expression
Seeking tools that yield

Hands that mould or draw or carve
Feet that go into the night
Mouths that speak in silences
Hearts that dare to feel

Tongues that sing or shout or not
Brains that plough
The hardened soil of set-down truths
Fingers that paint
Images in flight

And minds that weave stories
Oh stories!
Stories of victory, of joy, of completion
Of agony, of bitterness, of despair
Stories with sad endings …or no endings
Stories, stories.

4

MY BEGGING BOWL

It's early
Another day has dawned.
Another dark hopeless day.
I wonder
What purpose to one dreary day
following another?
What use of a succession
of useless, aimless days?

I sit up,
Stare around.
I'm tired, thirsty, hungry;
I'm hot, dirty, sticky.
I've not had a wash in days;
as even the heavens hold back
the sweet relief of rain.

I look around.
The world around me
is slowly waking.
Women go about
their early morning chores:
waking children, bathing them,
preparing breakfast…
People move about in a great

Hurry!
As if it matters,
as if anything matters.

I get up.
Might as well get a move on.
Might as well try to
scrape some existence.
I've long given up hope
of really living.
I pick my begging bowl
and start my rounds
Find a corner
And watch, and wait;
my eyes empty
my face blank.

(They begin.
They begin to drop money
Into my bowl,
five Naira, ten Naira, twenty Naira
with their minds elsewhere
and their eyes looking in the far horizon)

My bowl:
An opportunity to give alms,
a reservoir for their 'charity',
a balm to soothe their consciences,
a place to invest so that
they can get back
a full measure, pressed down,
shaken and running over.

We are dumped at the outskirts of town)
A woman passes by,
She looks at us: there are
tears, tears, endless tears
'What's your name?'
she asks me.

I laugh
Name? What name?
Whatever name I had been given
Withered and died long ago
from disuse.
'How long have you been begging?'

Time
How long?
How could I keep track?
Hours, weeks, years-
What did they matter?
One aimless day simply rolls into another
And one year gets lost in the next

Only one thing matters:
My begging bowl...

(First published in Spirituality. Vol 14; No 76. 2008)

5

One Fool Too Many

A third time you fell
Lover of Life and of all people
You kissed the ground again
The place of zero

Yes, Jesus, you fell
Back to the place where all ends.
And begins?
That place of humiliation.
Of shame. Of Failure

You fell - hard, rough
In fellowship with all those on the ground
Those whose faces are smeared with mud
Those who lives are 'down'

Jesus you fell again, a third time?
The first fall I could overlook
The second fall I could pity
But this third fall?
Invites my ridicule, mockery, judgement

'Seventy times seven' you told us
But this third fall is sometimes one too many
I can take only so much.
I can support the first fall.
Maybe the second.
But the third?
There is a limit to tolerance, Lord!
Or isn't there?

Help me Lord, Heal me
Of those times I give up
I resent the place of Zero
And desire to be where you have not put me.
When I resist starting again
Because I think I should have graduated.

Help me Lord, Heal Me
Of those times I walk past you,
Lying on the ground;
In those I know, or hear about.
Unable to forgive, to love, to reach out
Because you have fallen too many times
And my heart is not big enough.

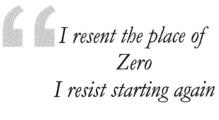

*I resent the place of
Zero
I resist starting again*

6

Resurrection Deferred

"Come my Beloved, come
At last the stone is rolled away.
Step forth in majesty
Out of the tomb of your old life
Into the magnificence of Newness"

Ah Lord! I have been waiting for ages
I am coming!
But Lord, could you widen
The entrance of the tomb?
My luggage cannot squeeze through

"Luggage? What luggage?"
Oh. Lord. These are sensitive, crucial files and folders
They contain key information and outline
For many activities
I have to bring them along
And with your Light, we can improve on them.

"Come on your own
The entrance is big enough for you

It is the eye of the needle,
Whatever cannot pass through
Is superfluous.
Come, Beloved. Just you."

You don't understand Lord
These files and books are important
And many people depend on
These roles and expressions
They need me to organize, support, animate

I am a card-carrying member
of the Complaints Party
And a delegate to the national reunion
I am on the executive board
of the Self Pity Forum,
We just finalized our three year strategic plan.
Our Chapter of the Grumbling Association
is hosting a provincial meeting
And I chair the "el-ow-see".

I mentor the Young Blamers League,
And we are organizing a fundraising activity
To raise money for capacity building
Of the members.

31

The Commentators Club
Is hosting its global biennial conference
In less than a month
And we are inducting new members.

The Universal Disagreement Seminar
Is starting tomorrow
And I am giving the keynote address
And facilitating a training for trainers' workshop.

How could I leave all these behind Lord?
I was hoping that with your Light and Wisdom
We could bring freshness into all these activities

So you see Lord?
You do understand, don't you?
You do…?

"My Beloved
My Heart and the apple of my eye
This entrance, out of your old life
Can only take you
You, only, do I want"

Oh Well, Lord.
Can we postpone my release?

Give me time,

Time to complete these events.

To do a proper hand-over

And pass these roles on to someone else.

Then I will come

I will Lord.

Then I will cross the threshold

And walk, live, love in your Light

I request a deferment, Lord

I cannot come to the Banquet just now

But I will

Of course I will!

And who knows,

This eye of the needle may be wider

The next time....

36

7

Amnesia

Heart and mind and soul.
All one tiny mass.
Then like the flaring forth
a burst, a birth;
then the evolution - separation and greater complexity.

The autonomy of each;
the nourishing of one; the neglect of the other.
The discordance in growth,
the amnesia of oneness;
the paralysis of connectedness,
the glorification of each:
One a giant; the other a genius
One remains a seed.

At last at twilight
the sun has gone down
The shadows cover the land;
the hue reveals only what needs to be seen.
Each sits in a self-made cage
at the threshold of what might have been.

There is no wholeness
only the rugged thirsty edges
where each had fit before
Before. Before.
Completion cannot happen alone,
each needs the others.
Each needs to give and receive
And receive. And receive.

Little by little
Nostalgia grows and grows
It morphs into restlessness
And matures and grows
And morphs into wings and legs
Moving towards one another
Guided only by the memory of what was.

Other voices softening into
Irrelevant whispers
A long process of re-becoming
Fueled by desire
And memory and summons
Until touching one another
They begin to give
And to receive. To receive. Receive
Each receiving fully.
Giving up. Giving in. Giving

The ends come together
They touch
The edges become brittle
They connect, they join up
Until the lines fade
and the oneness is complete
Full circle

Life is at its zenith
And so must end
To birth another.

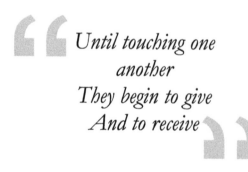

Until touching one
another
They begin to give
And to receive

8

There are neither certainties nor absolutes
Patterns haphazard like the moods of an infant
Years are but a moment, Events a scene
Blown away by winds of decision
Experiences an interlude
Washed off by waves of change

In the aftermath of the hurricane
We walk the ruins
The strange consolation of rubble
Grave of the familiar
We place our wreaths
And remember…

What are you God?
A puppeteer
Pulling strings at your whim?
You rob us of predictability
Stability is less than a mirage

Time plods on with boring monotony
Nostalgia an elusive bedmate
Hope and dreams reluctant guests
The timer is reset
We start all over at sunset

Life is re-defined

9

MY nEW
Market

I had a price tag for me
One on my back, one on my front
Some customers bought, some frowned;
Clients are too few, I said
They are abandoning me

Lower the prices, my advisers said
Don't be too demanding
And then you will have more
you will make merry
Then you will be happy

I changed all the price tags
To half price.
More customers came
Clients could easily afford me.
My stall was crowded
They were happy, grateful
And I was happy too.
Yes I was! I was. I was?

The moans began again:
Times are hard
Responsibilities crushing
We don't have much, we're indigent
Credit sales is the in-thing
If you want to stay open
You must sell on credit.

I did…and they trooped in
These customers, these regulars,
I could not let them down;
They had been loyal for years.
"See how blessed you are
You still have clients.
You are still open when
other shops have closed"

In the silence of one night
From the centre of the dark
The Voice asked,
'Are you fulfilled?'
Well, I have many clients
I am not alone,
I am not abandoned

'Are you whole?'
The Voice persisted
I am thankful, it could be worse
People are happy, friends are grateful
I am not alone,
I am not rejected

'Are you home, Beloved? Is this your worth?'
The Voice insisted.
At last I melted, I flowed into the Sacred.
The tears washed away the lies;
The volcano had erupted
And molten lava destroyed my illusions.
The deception was over

I don't know what 'whole' is;
I have forgotten how to be fulfilled.
Worth? What is that?
I don't know my way home
This here, this is all I know

Remember me---on my way
to Sodom and Gomorrah
My Beloved Abraham intercepted me
Bargaining, negotiating
He changed my value labels to price tags
From fifty to forty
To thirty, to ten

I yielded to the bargain
So that all Abraham's progeny will learn
that there is a value label
and there is a price tag.
Life will only ever offer you
What you ask for
No-one will up your price but you

Respect, honesty, love
Courtesy, fidelity, companionship
Reverence, integrity, justice.
These are not price tags dear
These are your due.
Value stickers that are
Non-negotiable, not bargain-able.

That night, in the silence,
before dawn
I tore down the credit labels
Peeled off all the price tags
Glued on my new value stickers
On everything that was me

In the morning
there was pandemonium
Customers raged, Regulars pleaded
Friends were shocked,
Advisors threatened,
"This is social suicide,
You won't survive!"

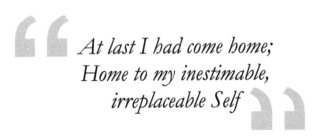

At last I had come home;
Home to my inestimable,
irreplaceable Self

But I laughed
The Voice had given me a revelation
Had exposed my self-betrayal
No-one could give me a price tag again
At last I had come home
Home to my inestimable, irreplaceable Self

The customers thinned out
My regulars became regular elsewhere
Loyal clients avoided me
Many debtors relocated
Epilogue is anti-climax

At any one time, now
There are only one or two in my shop
Precious, Priceless, Sincere people
No taking for granted, no exploitation
No bargaining, no underhand games

I have become a millionaire
To the power zillion.
Crowds who deal with price tags are out;
Select few who know true value are in.
I have created another market:

In my brand new world,
Supply meets sky-high demands.

10

Into the
Abyss

Spiralling into a bottomless abyss
in the middle of the sea,
at the speed of light.
I lose control
yet I know
'twas for this I was born.

I try to go back to familiar shores
but the wind blows my boat
forcefully away.
I taste fear yet I'm
secretly excited:
My life is at last beginning!

Old flames die out, new ones are kindled
Old loves lose their attraction
as the New beckons
with tantalizing sweetness.
I say, "Yes, yes. Yes, at last!"

Former swimming pools
seem no more than watering holes.

The wide rough sea calls with alarming
  Persistence:
invites me to danger, to risk, to LIFE!

How do I explain…
my restless spirit thirsts for adventure,
and 'home' for me is
the thick of the wilds
and the awesome unpredictability
of a simmering volcano?

How do I say
that 'inertia' and 'routine'
are for me synonyms of
prison and misery;
and 'never' and 'don't'
do to me
what salt does to the earthworm?

So I spiral into this abyss of the unknown
I choose this lonely path
remain true to my inner call.
For I know
only in this abyss
will I meet You face to face.

I choose this
lonely path
remain true
to
my inner call

Into the
Abyss

11

Frontlines

(For the 2020 Corona Virus pandemic)

Earth's layers have shifted
The universe has tilted
Our compasses no longer serve
We watch bewildered
As the frontlines proliferate

The health service providers
In the eye of the storm
Serving yet not understanding
This visitor that leaves
Confusion and death in its wake
Escaping all medical breakthroughs

The earth nurturers, farmers
Sowing and weeding and harvesting
Nourishing all without discrimination
Prey and predator
Vegan and carnivore

The marketers
Bringing essentials to the denizens
Making shopping possible
Keeping digestion and assimilation going

Strength for the voluntary
And involuntary tasks

The parents with the children
Keeping them home
Grandparents alone
Quarantining and cocooning
Getting to know each other in new ways
Staying indoors and keeping others homebound
Yes, that too is frontier

The frightened
Those who bear the burden of fear
For the rest of us
With hearts beating, dire images in dreams
Voicing our hidden cry: "Eloi, Eloi
Lama sabachthani".

The curious
Those who create and dispense freely
Conspiracy theories, Armageddon scenarios;
Fault finding and finger pointing.
They point us to the mystery
That every story is true
But none is complete -
No single move of any player
Equals the whole game

The brave
Who look the disaster in the face
And call it by all its names.
Yet give hope and love
And resilience to all and sundry

The media
Collecting the facts, designing them
Picking and sorting and disseminating
Deciding what to tell and what to hold back.
They too are part of the war effort.

Those who key in the data
And show us daily
The progress of The Curve
In episodes and seasons
We watch that line
And will, with all our might
That this protagonist
In the Covid Soap Opera
Meets it waterloo
Sooner than soon.

The mystics
Who go behind the scenes
And catch glimpses
of the hidden harmony:
The earth recovering
Compassion doubling
Birds singing
Squirrels burrowing

Rivers running clean
Hearts going deep
Lungs gulping fresh air
Illusions shattered
They who invite us
To a post-covid future
And keep the fire ablaze
Within these ashes.

Marthas who plant, serve, visit, call
Davids who jump, sing, play, run
The thinkers and the doers
The organizers and the helpers

The universe has indeed shifted
Frontlines erupt everywhere
In this battle,
The roles do differ
But we remain in One Big Unfolding.

Guard your post lovingly
Because every pull of your sling
Lands a fatal stone on the head
Of this Goliath.

The End is written
Our Victory is certain.
Preordained.
Done.

*...we
remain in
One Big
Unfolding*

Frontlines

(for the 2020 Corona Virus pandemic)

"*…our
wounds heal.
The scars
fade*"

And the bubble burst.

There are no absolutes.
In the end we are but earthen vessels.
Our words like the wind.
Our intentions temporary as morning dew.

A curse on those
who put their trust in humans;
chaff that is blown away.

God does not punish
our transgressions do.
Our disillusionment the atonement
For the folly of substituting the eternal with the transient.

Once more, tail between legs
We find our way back
Lonely, battered, prodigal

With neo wisdom
We close again the door
To the Holy of Holies

And with compunction
Worship the Eternal
In Spirit and Truth.

Until our wounds heal.
The scars fade
And the next bubble floats along.

On we jump
For another ride
To Nowhere

13

Coin
Lost?

She swept under the chairs,
She looked between the cushions
She checked behind the dresser
And even lifted the mattress.

She peered between the cracks
Rummaged the pockets of her skirts
Turned the linen cupboard inside out
And even shook out each shoe.

She Looked. She Waited. She Yearned.
She Prayed. She Enquired. She Thought.
She Bemoaned, She Lamented. She Grieved.
It's just one coin, they said. One of so many!

No, it isn't just a coin. Well…yes it is.
But my collection is not complete
I have one coin less…ten is not the same as nine
Its own space is empty.

Every life story in allegory.
We with our different lost coins:

Love, self-esteem, playfulness
Confidence, dignity, self-respect
And more...always more.

We take on too much or too little.
We start too early or not at all.
We live in lack, or insecurity.
We work too hard or play too wrong.
We are over-accountable or not.

And then we start The Search
Yearning for completeness
Seeking our lost treasure
In friends, in career choices or changes
In trips, in solitude, in new addresses.

In bosses, in children, in neighbours, inspouses
In examination scores, in self-help habits.
The quest fuels our choices.
All the time frantic- chasing, hunting,
Longing to find what is lost.

Count your blessings! they say.
But the empty space within whispers differently.
Think how lucky you are! they say.
But the sense of wholeness remains elusive

Until in the fullness of time
We drop into the depths of Silence.
In that nurturing Abyss
We at last see: we've been looking outside
for what was always within.
We've been yearning for who we always are.

We are the lost-ness and we are the finding
All the time beautifully whole
The Saint of Assisi was given this sight:
"That which you are looking for
is the one who is looking".

*"...All the time
beautifully
whole"*

14

The Ayes (Don't) have it!

At last…
the Global Conference had been loading
For over two years
This was the Game Changer.
Reflections. Discernment. Questionnaires.
Pre-meetings and organising commits.

This was it!
The Conference began
Great facilitation. Expert moderation
The flow of ideas was torrential
We discovered each state of affairs,
named those yet to be discovered.

Causes analysed carefully
issues diagnosed with clinical dexterity
Roots traced down every anthropological avenue
Culture, Biology, Spiritual milieu,
Historical timelines, the expansion of the planet,
the sexual revolution, the technological dragnet
We discovered associations,
made correlations.

The days came to weeks,
We broke into think tank groups
We were the Big Thinkers - critical and logical
No wasted sentiments
Gurus in every sphere of life
Social. Medical. Spiritual. Environmental.
Matching experience with knowledge

Recommendations were collated
Mandates were issued, proposals proffered
We had it made - it was a DD
An enviable Done Deal
This would go down in history
And Oh Yes - It did.

Five years later we went back
All of us but one.
No, he was not dead. Well not really
He smiled as we left for the airport
'See you on your return" he said to our mascot

Armed with sizzling biannual reports
We re-entered the 'arena'.
What a rewarding experience!
The airport lounge had two huge screens
With catch phrases from our conference
The driver of our hired ten-seater
Was whistling a tune
composed from one of our mandates.
Did he know who his passengers were?
Our faces contorted as we struggled not to smile.

On the streets, the old and not-so-old
wore gold embossed t-shirts
With quotes from our recommendations.
When the traffic lights turned red
A man brought his wares
cushions embroidered in perfect calligraphy
with the theme of the conference.

There was a large billboard
Inscripted with part of our communique
the message short, sharp and sweet.
Thousands of people had signed up
To promote these recommendations

Long interviews or breakfast meetings?
Not required!
It was obviously visible
Our conference had been the Tipping Point!
Our awareness and sensitization
had yielded a hundred-fold!
So many had signed up,
The scenario repeated in other countries

On our return, our stay-back colleague
Welcomed us with a smile
Everyone was talking all at once
He noticed me at a corner
Sipping water and staring unseeing
at a spot on the floor

Totally immune
to the excited exuberant conversations
that fell like clouds all around me.

He came over, held my hands
Our eyes met
Then I knew
That he knew
That I now knew.
Nothing had really happened,
Not where it mattered:

In the Control Room,
In that elusive Inner Universe
Where the Game is truly decided.
There, the control switches lay arrayed
Undiscovered and still unflicked.

15

The VISION

The gift is not given whole
The visionary must be artist,
detective, scientist, seamstress.
The delivery is done haphazardly
A shade today, a curve tomorrow
A hue in the dream, a glimpse in the market
Each piece is whole yet
Incomplete on its own
Needing the others
To attain fullness
No piece looks defective
Imagination. Patience.
A leaf today, a piece of granite five years later
Each piece longing for the others
The vision grows, it changes
Fire burns it, rain washes it
The sun dries it, the tears purify it
Is it a carving or a painting?
Is it pattern or a landscape?
Wood or marble?
Cloth or glass?
The 'or' disqualifies the question
The whole is not an 'or'
More than an 'and'
A function of its parts, not a sum

16

What colour is life?
Life is orange
Like the sun stepping out at dawn
With proud claim of the skies.
Life is orange with flecks of blue and white.

What colour is life?
Life is orange
Like hot coals at the fireplace
On a harmattan morning
A warm cosy embrace
Life is orange with shades of grey.

What colour is life?
Life is orange
A small orange dot
Surrounded by large black waves
Stifled and strangled
Life is orange
Struggling to live.

What colour is life?
Life is orange
Swollen like a ripe abscess
Waiting to burst
And spill its insides
Life is orange
With red in its belly.

What colour is life?
Life is orange
Dim and plain
Like a table cover
Weathered over time
Life is orange
Dying out.

What colour is life?
Life is orange
A ball in the twilight horizon
With bridesmaids in shades and tones
Leaving hope in its wake
Life is orange
Birthing the rainbow.

17

Through
Her
Eyes

She is deep and profound
delves into the deeps of things
discovers hidden meanings
concealed connections, exact expressions
Like an archaeologist,
she digs and filters, scrutinises and dates

She sees the deeper meaning of things
through the crystal ball of familiar patterns;
interprets relationships with
narrow margins of error
has insights into the hungers of life,
the yearnings of hearts,
the desires of souls.

She sees how the one truth
Manifests in multiple events
How the same light
Shines through different cracks
How the same air
is flavoured with different aromas

She sees with the inner eye
The loom from which
the different weaves emerge;

Through Her Eyes

The unacknowledged world
that is the fodder of dreams.
Like a forensic pathologist
She observes, waits, researches
To uncover the dots, connect them
Root out the evidence, interpret them.

Some days her looking
screeches to a shuddering halt
Downs its tools and refuses to cooperate
She begs, she threatens, she tantrums
She cajoles, she bargains, she raves
But its decision is hard
like set concrete

With the deceitful sham of time
She lets go, relaxes, drops into silence
She is remade by what is absent

Stripped of the gift
Of deeper sight
She begins to see
The kaleidoscope of Life
Manifesting each moment
Like a television with multiple channels
Of to-die-for programmes.

She sees the delicate topography of leaf veins
The curved paths of wrinkles on faces
The colour synchrony on butterfly wings
The ephemerality of a blink

She feels the textures of things
The smooth of silk, the rough of a tree's bark
The soft of baby skin
the wet of tears

She hears things
The undulating tone of wails
The high pitch of sirens
The perfect harmony of snoring
The loud silence of repressed emotions

She smells things
The sharp of compost
The faint tease of rain coming
The odour of old food
The scent of happy sweat
The fragrance of wet clay

When she stops looking
she learns to see
The magnificence everywhere
When she stops digging
she realises the surface
Is bursting with overt mystery
Perfect unfolding beauty
Imperceptible wonders
Miracles waiting to be gulped - a piece a moment.

Looking waits
Until seeing catches up
And together
They romp and relish
The mysterious unending expressions
In each moment

She testifies
Life is more than gift
It is -It just is
Beyond description
Beyond scrutiny
Larger than analysis
With more dots than could ever be connected.

Life offers itself endlessly
Asking only to be received
With every inch of our vast becoming
And poured out in turn
Through the myriad vents of our boundless being.

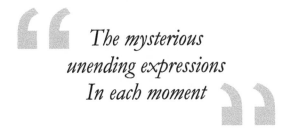

The mysterious
unending expressions
In each moment

18

Birthing
The
Soul

The door handle covered
with rags of all colours
I stepped over paint cans, dirty brushes, pieces of
   Canvas
Oil pastels littered my way.
The walls intended to be lilac
were now a decors' nightmare
I nearly slipped on an oily cloth
But caught the edge of the desk on time
My hand now baptised with a myriad of colours
She never lifted her head from the easel;
Pencils and brushes stuck in her hair, behind her ears
She wet her fingers with saliva
And softly caressed an edge of the canvas
Her face a rich salad of pain, joy, hope and the past
Birthing a part of her soul
Finally peeping over her shoulders
I gasped at the raw perfection…
"The face of God!"

"Come down the corridor
The last room on your left," she called
This could not be the kitchen,
More like a looter's left over
Surfaces littered with used dishes
Sinks piled with bowls and cutlery,
Flour on the stove, oil on the counter
Pots and pans in all stages of use
The scent of curry and thyme and bitter leaves
Chasing each other around the kitchen
And Mozart playing from an old CD player
Her head stuck in the oven.
The oven tray slid out
I gasped at the magnificent spread and saw....
"The face of God".

*Her face a rich
salad of pain,
joy, hope and the
past*

85

She screamed, tears rolling down her
cheeks
"I will never do this again!"
I tutted and soothed and she calmed down
Waiting in trepidation for another attack.
For the six hours and one
She gasped, and wailed, and cussed and moaned.
Her sweat oozed out, pain exploded
Her brows were mopped, her waist massaged;
The room filled with echoes of pain
There was blood, there was fluid, there was shit and
  piss.
She thrashed and gave a mighty shout -
Through the mess and bedlam, it glided out.
A lusty cry, fist clenched, eyes closed.
Through tear soaked eyes, I looked in wonder
Perfect and pure….
"The face of God".

19

Enticed

The song in our souls
We dance to it
The angels cheer us on,
The saints nod in rhythm.
We listen to the tune,
understand the beat
Move to its cadence.

We learn, we live.
We grow up
Become sensible and appropriate;
Our unused primal wisdom atrophies.
We no longer dance our music.
With the passing of time
It is replaced
by the cheers and accolades
Of a tone-deaf world.

Enticed by our giftedness,
we overlook our core nature.
Seduced by our abilities,
we ignore our essence.
Lured by our swiftness
We forget to dance.

But that inner music is dogged.
As we ignore it
It evolves and learns ways to survive.
In unguarded moments
When we listen to poetry
Or plant, or cook, or play.
In that twilight space
between sleep and wake
And wake and sleep

When we are alone
Intoxicated with sobriety
When we hold our first baby in our hands
When tragedy looms
And the tears stream unauthorised
Down our faces

In moments of sorrow,
Of graced sadness
The strains of our inner music play.
Then we remember
And remember when we forgot

We try to bury it
Like we would an irritating ringing phone
In the middle of clinching a deal.
With more success
ours, our children's, our country's, our race's
We try to drown out the music
With achieved goals. Or Liquor. Or games.
Or thought. Or crime. Or love…
They give us temporary reprieve;
They do.
But the music…is not going back mission-less

As the clock ticks and the years
disappear in a blink,
Our bodies go their natural way
inside and out.
Silence becomes less an enemy
Slowly. Slowly, we slowly see
That we are the dance of the music
Nothing sounds as sweet,
Nothing feels as familiar
As the music the universe played
As we entered it.

Our Music, our melody
Slowly we surrender to it
Coming home at last
And let the wordless music
At last be
We are willingly enticed
As our music accomplishes its mission
Through us
As us.
We are the dance
Of the universe.

Our children wonder who we now are
Our grandchildren delight in this dance
That seems to have skipped
a generation. Or more?

20

Prodigal Smile

like an orchestra conductor
The heart conducts the whole body
It sends a signal
and the whole body
Responds with gusto

when the heart smiles
Every member of the orchestra smiles
Effortlessly
A spectacular symphony
Such harmony

oftentimes
There is a schism
And the members of the orchestra
Declare autonomy
Take up self-rule
Smile when the heart hasn't
It is a distortion
An eye-sore
An emotional calamity

the mouth smiles
The eyes are deadly
The lips spread thin
The rest of the body is in
Stiff un-negotiable resistance

the teeth are exposed
The face is contorted
The muscles are confused
Because the signal from the
    conductor
And the action from the members
Are askew

the voice comes out sweet.
Attempting to compensate
It overshoots
And drips saccharine
In excess of the needs and demands.

only then does the smile hurt
A smile from the heart never hurts
Because the whole body supports it
Carries it, bears it, celebrates it.

the discomfort happens
when it leaves home
All on its own
Without the heart's blessing

a prodigal smile

21

WILD
BEAUTY

Oh you would
that the forest become a garden.
Cut the briars!
Remove the weeds!
Prune the trees!
Mow the grass!
Create Beauty

Yes you would
that the forest become a garden.
Plant the flowers.
Create a hedge.
Arrange the rows.
Design the shrubs.
Put a bench or two,
that people may come
and soak in the beauty.

I know you would
That the forest become a garden.
I wish you would learn
step by step

the beauty, the wild, terrible beauty
of the forest,
the deep mystery of the untame;
that you would
let the forest
draw out your spirit, your wild spirit.

That you would not tame
its virgin beauty;
that you would be you
amidst the trees, the thorns
the squirrels, the fallen leaves;
that the nests, the animal droppings
the bird song, the cricket screech
would call you
to the senseless abundance
and raw beauty of life.

Oh that you and the forest
would become one

Lightning Source UK Ltd.
Milton Keynes UK
UKHW010648300720
367419UK00001B/210